SOCIAL AGENCY SINGULARITY

The PREMISES Series

By

GHIZLANE OBTEL

ISBN: 9798304630764

Imprint: Independently Publish

By the Ever Free Me,

Fathoming the Nothingness

Into Architecture

And Engineering

The Emergence

Of the Transcendent Immune World

Of the Ever Free!

SOCIAL AGENCY

SINGULARITY

The PREMISES Series

By

GHIZLANE OBTEL

TABLE OF CONTENT

PRELUDE:

The journey to understanding Social Agency Singularity is a natural progression from the explorations undertaken in the preceding volumes of the Social Agency series. Each book has laid a cornerstone for this culminating discourse, examining how social agency operates as the fulcrum of individual and collective behavior, societal systems, governance structures, and the trajectory of civilizations. This prelude invites readers to reflect on the interconnectedness of the ideas presented in earlier works and how they converge to illuminate the profound implications of singularities within social agency systems.

The Foundations: Linking the Previous Volumes

1. Social Agency as Premise for Radicalization and Terrorism:

In the first book, Social Agency as Premise for Radicalization and Terrorism, we explored how individuals and groups harness their agency to pursue extreme ideologies. This volume dissected how disenfranchised or alienated individuals can weaponize their agency when societal systems fail to provide equitable opportunities for inclusion, purpose, and voice. It demonstrated how unchecked singularities in governance or justice systems can become breeding grounds for discontent, creating vacuums where radicalization thrives.

These insights underpin Social Agency Singularity by showing the dangerous consequences of singularities that marginalize individuals or segments of society. When singularities become entrenched, they exacerbate exclusion and frustration, laying the groundwork for societal fragmentation and, in extreme cases, violence.

2. Manual of Engineering Social Agency:

The second book, Manual of Engineering Social Agency, delved into the practical tools and frameworks for shaping social agency in ways that promote collective progress and harmony. It examined how societies can engineer social structures, roles, and narratives to align individual agency with the broader goals of civilization.

Yet, as Social Agency Singularity reveals, the engineering of social agency is not always neutral or equitable. Singularities arise when the mechanisms of engineering become tools of exclusion, control, or self-preservation for specific groups or institutions. This book serves as both a cautionary tale and a roadmap for reclaiming the constructive potential of engineered social agency.

3. Social Adaptation and Social Agency:

In *Social Adaptation and Social Agency*, we analyzed how individuals adapt within societal systems to maximize their agency, often navigating the constraints imposed by their environments. The book emphasized the dynamic interplay between personal choices and societal structures, highlighting how adaptation can either reinforce or resist oppressive systems.

Social Agency Singularity builds on this by examining what happens when the spaces for adaptation become closed or distorted.

Singularities, by their nature, limit the avenues for adaptation, forcing individuals and groups into rigid, inequitable frameworks that stifle growth and innovation. Understanding these limitations provides a lens through which to critique and reimagine societal structures.

4. Social Agency Science: The Universal Paradigm:

The fourth volume, Social Agency Science: The Universal Paradigm, offered a comprehensive theory of social agency as a universal principle governing human behavior, societal development, and governance systems. It posited that social agency is the thread linking personal autonomy to collective progress, providing the scaffolding for civilizations to thrive.

However, as Social Agency Singularity demonstrates, the universality of social agency is vulnerable to disruption. Singularities create fractures within this paradigm, replacing universality with insularity. This book extends the scientific framework of social agency by addressing its limitations and proposing strategies for overcoming the barriers imposed by singularities.

5. Social Truth:

The fifth book, *Social Truth*, investigated the complex relationship between societal narratives, power structures, and the lived realities of individuals. It revealed how distortions of truth—whether through propaganda, systemic bias, or the manipulation of language—can shape perceptions of justice, equality, and progress.

Social Agency Singularity takes this analysis further by exposing how these distortions create and sustain singularities. By redefining reality, singularities alter the foundational truths that underpin social cohesion and justice, creating systems that serve only themselves. This volume calls for a reassertion of universal truths to counteract the isolating and fragmenting effects of singularities.

The Central Premise of *Social Agency Singularity

In Social Agency Singularity, we confront a critical juncture where the very mechanisms designed to uphold justice, equity, and progress become tools of exclusion and self-preservation. Singularities emerge when institutions, ideologies, or individuals monopolize power and redefine systems to serve narrow interests, detaching themselves from the broader social contract. These singularities trap societies in loops of stagnation, injustice, and fragmentation, eroding the principles enshrined in documents like the Universal Declaration of Human Rights (UDHR).

Unlike the previous volumes, which emphasized the potential of social agency to drive progress and adaptation, this book delves into the darker side of this phenomenon. It exposes how the misuse or misalignment of social agency can create closed systems that resist accountability, suppress dissent, and perpetuate inequality. In doing so, Social Agency Singularity serves as both a critique of existing systems and a call to action for reform.

The Unified Vision: From Fragmentation to Integration

The exploration of singularities in this book is not merely a critique but an invitation to rethink and reimagine how social agency operates within societies. Singularities are not inevitable; they are the product of choices—choices made by individuals, institutions, and societies. By understanding the mechanisms that create and sustain them, we can identify pathways to dismantle these isolating structures and restore the universality of social agency.

This book connects the threads of the Social Agency series into a unified vision. It demonstrates that while social agency has the power to drive radicalization, adaptation, and truth, it also has the potential to heal divisions, bridge gaps, and foster collective progress. To achieve this, we must confront the singularities that threaten to undermine these possibilities and work toward systems that prioritize equity, justice, and collaboration.

A Prelude to Action

As we embark on the journey through Social Agency Singularity, it is vital to remember that the stakes are not abstract. They are deeply personal, affecting the lived realities of individuals and communities. The challenge before us is to move beyond critique and toward action—to dismantle the singularities that fragment our societies and to build systems that honor the full potential of social agency.

This prelude sets the stage for a critical examination of the singularities that shape our world and a call to reclaim the ideals of justice, equality, and universal progress. It is not merely a continuation of the ideas presented in the Social Agency series but a culmination—a clarion call to address the fractures in our systems and to work toward a future where social agency is not a tool of exclusion but a force for collective good.

INTRODUCTION

The concept of singularity often conjures images of technological thresholds, moments when advancements in artificial intelligence or innovation render the old ways of doing things obsolete. But this book introduces a different kind of singularity—a social agency singularity. This is not about machines surpassing human capabilities; it is about human systems, institutions, and power structures reaching a critical point where they cease to function in service of the greater good, locking society into cycles of stagnation, oppression, or selective justice.

The social agency singularity represents the moment when the tools and mechanisms of governance, law, education, and leadership become self-serving rather than universally just. It describes a state where systems that should empower individuals and societies are instead monopolized by localized ideologies, interests, or power groups, isolating them from the universal principles of justice, equality, and the Universal Declaration of Human Rights (UDHR).

This book explores the pervasive phenomenon of the social agency singularity and its profound implications for societies striving for progress and cohesion. It examines how executive bodies, governance structures, leadership hierarchies, and legal frameworks can fragment, becoming entrenched in silos that work against their intended purpose. The singularity arises when these systems fail to adapt to the needs of the people they are meant to serve, perpetuating inequality, stifling innovation, and alienating entire populations from their rights and freedoms.

The Essence of Social Agency

At its core, social agency is the ability of individuals, groups, and institutions to act within their environment to influence outcomes, shape decisions, and create change. It encompasses the power to adapt, respond, and take responsibility for the well-being of society. Social agency thrives in systems that are open, collaborative, and guided by the principles of fairness and equality.

However, when social agency is distorted—when institutions prioritize their survival, internal ideologies, or self-interest over the public good—it leads to singularities. These singularities represent points where systems no longer function as they should, becoming closed, oppressive, and resistant to reform. Instead of advancing the collective well-being, they serve narrow interests, locking societies into patterns of injustice, inefficiency, and inequality.

The Rise of the Singularity

This book identifies and analyzes the key areas where singularities manifest in modern societies:

1. Executive Singularities: Institutions like school boards, law enforcement agencies, and corporations that operate as isolated entities, enforcing their own rules and standards without accountability to universal principles of justice.

2. Governance Singularities: Governments that become fragmented, with localized institutions dictating policy and law, subverting democratic processes and national unity.

3. Authority Figures Singularities: Leaders who lack the personal qualities required for effective governance, resorting to control, oppression, or monopolization of power to maintain their authority.

4. Change Singularities: Societies locked in cycles of stagnation and fragmentation, unable to enact meaningful change or advance collective progress.

These singularities do not arise in a vacuum. They are the result of systemic failures, ideological entrenchments, and the inability or unwillingness of institutions to adapt to the changing needs of society. As these singularities proliferate, they undermine the very foundations of democracy, justice, and human rights, creating a reality where the ideals enshrined in the UDHR exist only on paper, not in practice.

The Consequences of the Singularity

The singularity has far-reaching consequences for individuals, communities, and nations. It fragments society into isolated factions, each pursuing its own interests at the expense of the greater good. It perpetuates cycles of inequality and injustice, with some groups enjoying privileges and protections while others are marginalized or excluded. It stifles innovation and progress, as the systems designed to foster creativity and collaboration become rigid and self-serving.

The most devastating consequence of the singularity is the erosion of trust. When institutions fail to deliver justice, fairness, and opportunity, people lose faith in the systems meant to serve them. This loss of trust breeds disillusionment, apathy, and polarization, further entrenching the singularity and making it even harder to break free.

The Path Forward

Despite its challenges, the singularity is not an insurmountable barrier. This book argues that by understanding the mechanisms that sustain singularities, we can identify pathways to reform and renewal. Breaking free from the singularity requires systemic change, visionary leadership, and a shared commitment to the principles of justice, equality, and human rights.

Key strategies for overcoming the singularity include:

1. Reconnecting Institutions to Universal Principles: Ensuring that all systems operate under a common legal and ethical framework aligned with the UDHR.

2. Promoting Transparency and Accountability: Holding institutions and leaders accountable for their actions and decisions, and fostering a culture of openness and trust.

3. Encouraging Collaboration and Interconnection: Breaking down silos and fostering cross-sector cooperation to address societal challenges holistically.

4. Empowering Inclusive Leadership: Promoting leaders who possess the skills, vision, and integrity to guide societies toward collective progress.

5. Fostering a Culture of Adaptation and Resilience: Embracing flexibility and innovation to respond to changing needs and emerging opportunities.

Why This Book Matters

The concept of the social agency singularity is both timely and urgent. As societies around the world grapple with complex challenges—from inequality and polarization to climate change and technological disruption—understanding the forces that undermine collective progress is essential. This book provides a framework for analyzing these forces, offering insights and solutions for creating systems that are more just, equitable, and resilient.

By shining a light on the singularities that threaten the fabric of society, this book aims to inspire action and spark change. It challenges readers to confront the systemic flaws that perpetuate injustice and inequality, and to envision a future where social agency is not a privilege for the few, but a right for all.

Conclusion

Social Agency Singularity is not just a critique of the present; it is a call to action. It invites readers to examine the systems and structures that shape their lives and to demand better from the institutions and leaders entrusted with their well-being. It is a reminder that progress is not inevitable, but the result of deliberate effort, courage, and commitment to the greater good.

The journey to break free from the singularity is not easy, but it is necessary. By understanding the nature of the singularity and the pathways to overcome it, we can build a future that upholds the ideals of justice, equality, and human rights—one where the promise of social agency is fulfilled for all.

CHAPTER 1:
THE POWER OF WORD DEFINITION

Language is the vessel through which societies construct meaning, identity, and systems of governance. Words are not just passive tools for communication; they are active agents of change and control. A single definition of a word can ripple through history, shaping ideologies, laws, and social structures. In this chapter, we explore how the definition of one word can determine the course of an entire era, using the concept of "bias" as an illuminating example.

1. The Universal Nature of Bias

Bias, in its most universal and logical sense, refers to the subjective inclinations inherent in all individuals. It is a product of personal experiences, preferences, and limitations, making it a shared human trait. When bias is defined as universal, it encourages a level playing field before the law. Everyone is recognized as susceptible to bias, and legal systems can address it as a neutral concept, without targeting specific groups.

This universal understanding has profound implications. It emphasizes shared human fallibility, promotes dialogue, and fosters accountability. By acknowledging that everyone has biases, systems can focus on mitigating these tendencies through checks and balances, rather than vilifying particular groups.

2. The Identity-Based Definition of Bias

When the definition of bias shifts from a universal concept to one rooted in identity, it becomes a weaponized term. Under this redefinition, bias is no longer a shared human trait but an inherent flaw attributed to specific groups. This redefinition fractures societies by positioning one group as perpetually guilty and another as perpetually victimized.

For example, if a society accepts that one group is inherently biased against another, this creates a structural imbalance. The group labeled as biased is burdened with a perpetual accusation that influences how laws are interpreted and applied. In such a framework, the Human Rights Code, which is meant to apply universally, becomes a tool for enforcing this artificial division.

The implications are staggering. This redefinition creates a narrative where guilt and victimhood are preordained based on identity rather than individual actions or intentions. Legal, social, and cultural systems begin to operate on the premise of inherent guilt, demanding restitution and resource transfers from one group to another.

3. Legal and Institutional Distortions

The next step in this distortion involves embedding these definitions into legal and institutional frameworks. Legal texts, once designed to be neutral and universally applicable, are reinterpreted or blocked from applying unless they align with the identity-based narrative. Laws that were meant to ensure fairness are transformed into tools for enforcing perpetual restitution from one group to another.

This process undermines the foundational principle of equality before the law. Instead of focusing on individual behavior and evidence, legal systems operate on presumptions dictated by the distorted definition of bias. Over time, these presumptions become self-reinforcing, as legal precedents and societal norms evolve to reflect the distorted framework.

4. Erasing History and Constitutional Foundations

The third level of this distortion involves erasing historical and constitutional texts. History and law are reframed as products of "colonization" or systemic oppression, invalidating them as sources of universal principles. Instead, the distorted definition of bias becomes the sole reference for determining truth and justice.

By erasing historical context and foundational legal texts, societies lose their grounding in universal principles. The narrative of perpetual bias reshapes how societies think, work, and uphold the law. It becomes the lens through which all actions are judged, and any dissent is framed as further evidence of inherent bias.

5. The Consequences of a Single Word Distortion

When one word's definition is distorted, the consequences are far-reaching. The transfer of power, authority, and resources becomes an engineered mechanism, justified by the redefined term. Society's very structure shifts, as the distorted definition influences education, policy-making, and public discourse.

The case of bias illustrates a broader truth: the power of word definitions lies in their ability to shape reality. Words are the foundation of legal systems, societal norms, and collective identity. When their meanings are manipulated, the structures built upon them are likewise transformed.

6. Guarding Against Distortions

To prevent such distortions, societies must actively safeguard the integrity of language. This involves maintaining clear and consistent definitions, rooted in universal principles rather than transient ideologies. It requires vigilance against attempts to weaponize words for political or social control.

Language must remain a tool for understanding and uniting, not dividing and dominating. By recognizing the power of word definitions, societies can resist manipulation and ensure that words serve their intended purpose: fostering clarity, fairness, and progress.

In subsequent chapters, we will explore additional examples of how word definitions have shaped eras, movements, and civilizations, and how redefining them can either liberate or constrain humanity.

CHAPTER 2: PRIVILEGE, POWER, AND POLITICS

Language has always been a tool of immense power, capable of shaping ideologies, influencing societal structures, and redefining entire civilizations. Among the words that have gained prominence in modern discourse, "privilege" stands as a striking example of a term whose evolving definition has been used to disguise a larger ideological plan to reshape society.

This chapter explores how the term "privilege" can be weaponized to justify policies and actions that favor one group while systematically disempowering others. It examines the ways this redefinition impacts wealth, meritocracy, universal rights, and social cohesion, culminating in an analysis of the dangerous trajectory society takes when words are transformed into ideological instruments.

1. Privilege as a Weapon of Redistribution

At its core, "privilege" originally referred to advantages granted to some but not to others, often tied to wealth, status, or access. However, in modern usage, the term has evolved into a tool for labeling and targeting specific groups, often with the implicit goal of transferring resources, power, and status from one group to another.

When the word "privilege" is invoked, it is frequently linked to resources, positions, or opportunities that another group desires. For instance, wealth and prosperity, once symbols of hard work and achievement, are reframed as symbols of shame. Those who succeed are labeled "privileged," while others are deemed "underprivileged," creating a moral imperative to redistribute wealth and resources without examining the underlying causes of disparity.

This ideological reframing subtly redefines prosperity and success not as outcomes of effort or merit but as conditions of guilt. Those labeled as "privileged" are made to feel complicit in systemic inequality, even if their success is the result of personal achievement rather than inherited advantage.

2. The Attack on Meritocracy

Meritocracy, the principle of rewarding competence and hard work, is another casualty of the redefinition of "privilege." Under this framework, merit itself is reframed as oppressive. The skills, qualifications, and efforts required to excel in professions—such as surgeons, pilots, or engineers—are dismissed as barriers to equality.

This redefinition poses profound risks, especially in fields where competence is critical to safety and well-being. By equating merit-based selection with systemic exclusion, society risks diluting standards in critical professions. The consequences of such a shift are far-reaching, from diminished trust in institutions to life-threatening incompetence in essential services.

The narrative of privilege transforms competence from a virtue into a vice, undermining the foundations of fairness, excellence, and accountability. It prioritizes identity-based claims over objective qualifications, creating systems where identity supersedes ability.

3. Universal Rights Reframed as Exclusive

Universal rights, enshrined in documents like the Declaration of Human Rights and Freedoms, are meant to apply equally to all individuals. Yet, when viewed through the lens of "privilege," these rights are recast as exclusive benefits enjoyed by specific groups.

This redefinition justifies systematic disqualification of certain individuals or groups from accessing their universal rights. For example, freedom of speech, association, and due process may be denied to those labeled as "privileged" on the grounds that their rights perpetuate inequality. Simultaneously, these rights are championed as inviolable for those deemed "underprivileged."

The result is a two-tiered system of justice, where laws and protections serve only those who fit the narrative of oppression. This undermines the principle of equality before the law, eroding trust in legal systems and creating a society where rights are no longer universal but selectively applied.

4. Historical and Religious Beliefs as Targets

The ideological weaponization of privilege extends to history and religion. Historical narratives are reframed to portray "privileged" groups as oppressors, erasing their contributions and casting them as obstacles to progress.

Similarly, religious beliefs—such as the idea of a "chosen" status—are recast as privileges to be stripped away. This ideological shift seeks to deconstruct and delegitimize the spiritual, cultural, and historical foundations of certain groups, using the guise of correcting historical injustices.

By discrediting the historical and cultural identities of targeted groups, the ideology of privilege ensures that only its narrative remains dominant. This creates a cultural vacuum where the past is erased, and new generations are educated in a one-sided ideology devoid of historical nuance or critical analysis.

5. The Consequences of Ideological Restructuring

The systematic use of "privilege" to justify resource redistribution and social restructuring has profound consequences:

- **Wealth as Shame:** Success and prosperity are reframed as moral failings, discouraging ambition and undermining economic growth.

- **Meritocracy as Oppression:** Competence and qualifications are devalued, leading to declining standards in critical fields.

- **Rights as Tools of Exclusion:** Universal rights are selectively applied, creating a fractured and unjust legal system.

- **History Erased:** Historical narratives are rewritten to support the ideological framework, silencing dissent and critical thought.

At its core, this redefinition is driven by jealousy and resentment. It transforms legitimate advocacy for justice and equality into a zero-sum game where one group's gain is another's loss. By institutionalizing these dynamics, society risks descending into chaos, disintegration, and anarchy.

6. The Legal Loophole and Its Ramifications

The use of legal systems to enforce this ideological restructuring exacerbates the problem. Under the guise of "protected statuses" and human rights codes, laws are reinterpreted to favor identity-based claims over fairness and due process.

This creates a legal loophole where wealth, power, and privilege are transferred not through merit or justice but through identity. The legal system, once a guarantor of equality and fairness, becomes a tool of systematic redistribution based on ideological narratives.

The result is a society where trust in institutions collapses, and civil unrest becomes inevitable. Without a fair and impartial legal system, social cohesion disintegrates, paving the way for authoritarianism or anarchy.

7. A Warning for Future Generations

If new generations are educated within this ideological framework, the consequences will be catastrophic. By locking education into a one-sided narrative, society eliminates critical thinking, historical context, and logical analysis.

A society that prioritizes ideological conformity over truth and fairness cannot sustain itself. The legal and cultural foundations that support democracy, equality, and justice will erode, leaving chaos in their wake.

Conclusion

The weaponization of "privilege" is not merely a rhetorical shift but a profound ideological transformation. It disguises systemic jealousy and resentment as a quest for justice, creating a new regime of legalized redistribution and oppression.

By recognizing and resisting these manipulations, societies can preserve the principles of fairness, merit, and universal rights. The true test of any society is its ability to balance justice with equality, and to ensure that language remains a tool for progress rather than a weapon of division.

CHAPTER 3:
TRANSFER OF ROYAL STATUS

Language, when manipulated, can become the catalyst for profound social and political transformations. Among the most devastating effects of such manipulation is the creation of a new social hierarchy, resembling a monarchy, in which one group attains enduring privilege at the expense of others. Through a combination of neuro-linguistic programming (NLP), legal distortions, and generational re-education, the concept of "privilege" can be reframed to justify a permanent redistribution of wealth, status, and power.

This chapter explores the process by which a single word and its distorted definition can result in the establishment of a new societal structure: one where a specific group enjoys a de facto royal status. This "transfer of royal status" is not overtly proclaimed but becomes the lived reality of a society reshaped by laws, norms, and education systems designed to perpetuate this new hierarchy.

1. The Linguistic Genesis of Royal Status

The foundation of this societal transformation lies in the deliberate reframing of privilege as an inherent, identity-based condition. Certain groups are labeled as perpetually "privileged" based on historical narratives, while others are deemed "oppressed" and deserving of perpetual restitution.

Through this linguistic game, privilege ceases to be a neutral descriptor of advantages that can be earned, lost, or shared. Instead, it becomes a moral indictment and a justification for transferring wealth, status, and power. This process is rooted in:

- **Historical Alienation:** Revising history to portray one group as consistently oppressive and another as eternally victimized.

- **Legal Reinterpretation:** Crafting laws that systematically favor one group while disqualifying others under the guise of rectifying historical wrongs.

- **Generational Indoctrination:** Educating new generations in narratives devoid of historical nuance, logical validity, or legal impartiality, ensuring the perpetuation of the status quo.

This linguistic and ideological reprogramming lays the groundwork for the transfer of royal status from historically recognized authorities to a new identity-based elite.

2. The New Structure of Privilege

Once the linguistic reframing is established, societal structures begin to shift toward a new form of privilege. The characteristics of this new status are as follows:

1. Legal Privilege in Perpetuity: The privileged group is granted legal protections and advantages that remain in effect indefinitely, under the justification of correcting historical wrongs.

2. Guaranteed Resource Transfer: Wealth and authority are continuously redirected to this group through laws, policies, and societal norms. These transfers are framed as restitution but operate without time limits or mechanisms for reassessment.

3. Codified Allowances: Systems are established to provide ongoing benefits—financial, legal, or social—to the privileged group, resembling the allowances granted to royalty.

4. Perpetual Execution: The redistribution of privilege and resources becomes a constant societal function, embedded in institutions and cultural practices.

Through these mechanisms, the privileged group effectively gains a generational status that mirrors hereditary aristocracy or royalty.

3. The Role of Social Agency

The establishment of this new status relies heavily on mobilizing every margin of social agency. Individuals and institutions are co-opted into recognizing and enforcing the privileged group's elevated status. This involves:

- **Legal Enforcement:** Laws are crafted and interpreted to prioritize the privileged group's claims, often at the expense of fairness or due process.

- **Cultural Reinforcement:** Media, education, and public discourse are used to normalize the new hierarchy, presenting it as morally and historically justified.

- **Institutional Participation:** Organizations, businesses, and governments align their policies to reflect the new status quo, further entrenching the privileged group's dominance.

The result is a society where the privileged status becomes an unspoken yet omnipresent reality, shaping every interaction, decision, and institution.

4. The Emergence of a De Facto Monarchy

As this system evolves, it begins to resemble a constitutional monarchy in which the privileged group occupies the role of royalty. This new "royal status" is characterized by:

- **Hereditary Privilege:** The privileged status is tied to identity and passed down through generations, much like hereditary monarchy.

- **Unequal Application of Laws:** Legal protections and benefits are disproportionately available to the privileged group, creating a two-tiered system of justice.

- **Cultural Reverence:** The group is elevated in cultural narratives, portrayed as deserving of its status due to historical victimization.

This transformation fundamentally undermines the principles of democracy, equality, and universal rights. What emerges is an empire for the few, where the law and society are mobilized to sustain the privileged group's dominance.

5. The Role of Neurolinguistic Programming

The power of this transformation lies in its subtlety. Through NLP techniques, words and phrases are redefined to create a new reality:

- **Privilege** becomes synonymous with guilt, erasing the nuances of individual achievement or circumstance.

- **Justice** is reframed as the perpetual redress of historical wrongs, prioritizing identity over fairness.

- **Equality** is replaced with equity, demanding unequal treatment to achieve outcomes deemed fair by the privileged group.

These linguistic shifts are embedded in legal and educational systems, ensuring their longevity and effectiveness.

6. The Social and Legal Consequences

The transfer of royal status has profound implications for society:

- **Disintegration of Meritocracy:** By prioritizing identity over competence, critical institutions lose their effectiveness and legitimacy.
- **Erosion of Universal Rights:** Laws and protections become tools for enforcing privilege rather than ensuring equality.

- **Social Fragmentation:** The perpetual elevation of one group fosters resentment and division, undermining social cohesion.

- **Loss of Historical Truth:** Rewriting history to justify the new hierarchy deprives society of the lessons and wisdom needed to navigate the future.

The legal and societal structures created to sustain this status ultimately lead to chaos, as the principles of fairness, justice, and merit are replaced by arbitrary identity-based claims.

7. Educating Future Generations

The final piece of this system is the education of future generations. By teaching one-sided narratives and suppressing critical thinking, the privileged group ensures the perpetuation of its status.

Without access to historical truths, logical scrutiny, or legal impartiality, new generations grow up accepting the new hierarchy as natural and inevitable. This erases any hope of challenging or reforming the system, locking society into a perpetual state of inequality and dysfunction.

Conclusion

The transfer of royal status is a cautionary tale about the power of words and their ability to reshape societies. When a single word, such as "privilege," is distorted to justify systemic redistribution, the result is a new form of monarchy that undermines the principles of democracy and equality.

By recognizing and resisting these manipulations, societies can protect their foundational values and ensure that language remains a tool for progress rather than oppression. The lesson is clear: the redefinition of words can transform not only laws and institutions but the very fabric of social reality.

CHAPTER 4: PYRAMIDS DECODED AS LAW SINGULARITY

The concept of a pyramid has long been symbolic of hierarchies in society, representing a concentrated apex of power supported by broader, subordinate layers. When applied to the social and legal structures of modern societies, the pyramid becomes a metaphor for a disturbing reality: the creation of a hierarchy in which wealth, power, influence, authority, and resources are systematically locked into one group in perpetuity.

This chapter unpacks how such pyramidal structures emerge when laws, constitutions, and the Declaration of Universal Human Rights (DUHR) are hijacked and redefined to serve a singular purpose: the continuous empowerment and enrichment of one group at the expense of all others. Through mechanisms of legal singularity and social agency singularity, these systems create a new societal reality where the law ceases to be a universal protector and instead becomes a tool for perpetuating inequality.

1. The Law as the Apex of Power

In an ideal society, the law is a neutral framework designed to uphold justice, equality, and fairness for all. However, when the law is hijacked and restructured to serve the interests of a single group, it becomes the apex of a pyramidal hierarchy:

- **Legal Capture:** Laws are rewritten, interpreted, or selectively enforced to prioritize the interests of the privileged group.

- **Constitutional Distortion:** Foundational principles, such as equality before the law, are undermined to create exceptions and privileges for the apex group.

- **Perpetual Enforcement:** The legal system is transformed into a self-reinforcing mechanism that sustains the hierarchy indefinitely.

This process locks society into a structure where the law no longer serves its original purpose but instead becomes a tool for maintaining and expanding the power of the privileged few.

2. The First Law Singularity

The "law singularity" occurs when the legal system is no longer impartial or universally applicable but is instead absorbed into a singular purpose: the continuous service of one group. This singularity has several defining characteristics:

1. Monopolization of Legal Power: The group at the apex gains exclusive control over the creation, interpretation, and enforcement of laws.

2. Erosion of Universal Rights: Rights and protections are selectively applied, favoring the apex group while excluding others.

3. Inverted Justice: The law shifts from being a shield for the vulnerable to being a weapon against those outside the privileged group.

This singularity creates a system where the law becomes a "battery" for sustaining the power of the apex group, draining its effectiveness for everyone else.

3. The Social Agency Singularity

Parallel to the law singularity is the emergence of a "social agency singularity," where the mechanisms of social influence and power are similarly captured. Social agency—the ability of individuals or groups to act and make meaningful changes in society—is concentrated at the top of the pyramid, leaving the majority disempowered.

This is achieved through:

- **Cultural Hegemony:** Media, education, and public discourse are controlled to reinforce the privileged group's narrative and suppress dissent.

- **Institutional Domination:** Key institutions, such as academia, corporations, and governments, are co-opted to align with the apex group's interests.

- **Systemic Disempowerment:** Marginalized groups are systematically stripped of their ability to challenge or reform the system.

The result is a society where social agency is monopolized by the apex group, leaving others with limited or no capacity to influence their circumstances.

4. The Pyramidal Hierarchy of Social Reality

When the law and social agency are captured in this way, society is transformed into a pyramidal hierarchy. This structure has distinct layers:

1. The Apex: The privileged group, enjoying perpetual legal and social advantages.

2. The Enforcers: Institutions and individuals who benefit from maintaining the system, such as bureaucracies, media, and select allies of the apex group.

3. The Subordinates: The majority of society, whose rights and opportunities are systematically curtailed.

4. The Excluded: Marginalized groups who are entirely excluded from the system and face systemic oppression.

This hierarchy ensures that power, wealth, and influence flow upward, concentrating at the apex while being drained from the lower layers.

5. Locking the Hierarchy into Perpetuity

The perpetuation of this pyramidal structure is achieved through several mechanisms:

- **Legal Inheritance:** Laws and policies are designed to ensure that privileges are passed down through generations within the apex group.

- **Educational Indoctrination:** Schools and universities propagate narratives that justify and normalize the hierarchy.

- **Economic Redistribution:** Wealth and resources are continually redirected to the apex group through taxation, reparations, or other mechanisms.

- **Cultural Reinforcement:** The apex group's status is celebrated and protected in cultural narratives, making challenges to the hierarchy socially unacceptable.

These mechanisms create a self-sustaining system where the hierarchy becomes the default reality for future generations.

6. The Effects of the Law Singularity

The consequences of this law singularity are profound:

- **Erosion of Democracy:** The concentration of power at the apex undermines democratic principles and institutions.

- **Loss of Social Mobility:** The hierarchy becomes rigid, preventing individuals from rising above their assigned layer.

- **Social Fragmentation:** Resentment and division grow among the lower layers, leading to unrest and instability.

- **Systemic Inefficiency:** By prioritizing identity over competence, the system loses its ability to function effectively.

Ultimately, the law singularity leads to a society that is neither just nor sustainable.

7. Decoding the Pyramid

To unravel this structure, it is essential to decode the mechanisms that sustain it:

1. Reclaiming the Law: Restoring the impartiality and universality of the legal system is critical. This includes revisiting laws that perpetuate privilege and ensuring equal application of justice.

2. Restoring Social Agency: Empowering individuals and groups to act and influence society requires dismantling the cultural and institutional barriers that sustain the hierarchy.

3. Promoting Historical Truth: Countering narratives that justify the pyramid with accurate, nuanced accounts of history is essential for breaking the cycle of generational indoctrination.

4. Fostering Meritocracy: Reestablishing competence and merit as the primary criteria for advancement can help rebuild trust and efficiency in institutions.

These steps are necessary to dismantle the pyramid and create a society that is truly equitable and just.

Conclusion

The pyramidal hierarchy of law and social agency represents a fundamental distortion of the principles of justice and equality. By locking wealth, power, and influence into the hands of a privileged few, it creates a society where the law serves as a tool of oppression rather than protection.

Decoding and dismantling this pyramid requires a concerted effort to reclaim the universality of the law, restore social agency to all individuals, and challenge the narratives that sustain the hierarchy. Only then can society move beyond the singularity of law and social agency and toward a future where justice and equality are not just ideals but realities.

CHAPTER 5: THE POWER OF SELF-IMAGE ON IDENTITY

Self-image is a foundational component of individual and collective identity. It influences not only how people view themselves but also how they interact with the world and their role within society. When an ideology disguised as "justice for the underserved" manipulates self-image across generations, it becomes one of the most insidious tools for controlling social structures, perpetuating inequality, and reshaping the cultural landscape.

This chapter explores how this ideological framework alienates generations from their intrinsic truth, rewrites identities to fit a hierarchical narrative, and creates a societal order in which one group is exalted as inherently deserving of dominance while others are relegated to perpetual servitude.

1. Alienation from Truth and Identity

The ideology begins by reshaping the self-image of the group it deems "privileged." Through education, cultural narratives, and systemic reinforcement, individuals within this group are conditioned to see themselves as inherently flawed, shameful, and responsible for systemic injustices, regardless of their personal actions or merits.

- **Generational Guilt:** This ideology drills into children and young adults the belief that their identity is tied to a legacy of oppression, framing them as perpetual wrongdoers who must atone through servitude.

- **Identity Erosion:** Pride in one's cultural, historical, or familial heritage is systematically replaced with feelings of guilt and shame. The narrative positions these traits as symbols of privilege rather than as sources of strength or identity.

- **Self-Silencing:** The internalization of guilt leads individuals to suppress their voices, disengage from societal debates, and accept diminished roles as a form of penance.

This alienation disrupts the natural development of a healthy self-image, severing individuals from their truth and their right to participate fully and equally in society.

2. Elevating the "New Chosen Group"

Simultaneously, the ideology elevates another group as deserving of uncritical support, systemic favoritism, and the monopoly of legal and social advantages. This process involves a sophisticated linguistic and psychological framework designed to cement their status as morally and legally superior.

- **Narrative Dominance:** The identity of the "new chosen group" is portrayed as inherently virtuous, victimized, and deserving of restitution. This narrative silences scrutiny and fosters unquestioning acceptance of their privileged position.

- **Law as Servitude:** Legal frameworks are manipulated to favor this group, ensuring they are insulated from accountability while benefiting from systemic advantages. These laws are framed as corrections of historical injustice, but they function as mechanisms of exploitation.

- **Moral Monopoly:** This group is positioned as the ultimate moral authority, allowing their actions to go unchallenged while discrediting dissent as bigotry or ignorance.

This identity construction enables the new dominant group to exploit legal and social structures without resistance, cloaking their privilege in the language of justice and equality.

3. Normalizing the New Order

A crucial element of this ideological framework is its ability to assimilate new generations into believing that the imposed hierarchy is natural, just, and ideal. Through education, cultural reinforcement, and social conditioning, the new order is normalized and perpetuated.

- **Educational Indoctrination:** Schools and universities embed this narrative into curricula, teaching children from an early age that this hierarchy is the correct and just way of organizing society.

- **Cultural Saturation:** Media, literature, and entertainment reinforce the narrative by glorifying the dominant group and vilifying or marginalizing others.

- Behavioral Conditioning: Social rewards and punishments are structured to encourage compliance with the new order. Those who conform are celebrated, while dissenters face ostracism and condemnation.

Over time, this normalization erodes the ability of individuals to question or challenge the system, creating a society that willingly accepts inequality as the status quo.

4. Institutionalizing Perpetual Servitude

The culmination of this ideological framework is the establishment of a societal order in which one group is enshrined as dominant by law, history (as rewritten), and cultural consensus, while others are relegated to perpetual servitude.

- **Legal Perpetuity:** Laws are designed to institutionalize the dominance of the chosen group, ensuring that their privileged status is inherited by future generations.

- **Historical Revisionism:** History is rewritten to validate this hierarchy, erasing narratives that challenge the legitimacy of the dominant group's position.

- **Social Stasis:** Mobility within the hierarchy is systematically obstructed, ensuring that the lower layers remain subservient.

This new order is self-reinforcing, as the legal, cultural, and historical mechanisms supporting it are designed to prevent dissent or reform.

The Impact on Society

The generational impact of this distortion of self-image and identity is profound:

1. Erosion of Individual Agency: Individuals from the "privileged" group lose their sense of agency and worth, viewing themselves as inherently flawed and undeserving.

2. Fragmentation of Society: The creation of rigid hierarchies based on manipulated identities fosters division and resentment, weakening social cohesion.

3. Stagnation of Meritocracy: By prioritizing identity over competence, society loses its ability to innovate, progress, and address challenges effectively.

4. Loss of Justice: The legal and social systems, once designed to protect all individuals equally, become tools for perpetuating inequality.

Reclaiming Self-Image and Identity

To counter this devastating impact, it is essential to reclaim authentic self-image and identity through:

- **Restoration of Historical Truth:** Accurate, inclusive narratives must replace distorted accounts of history to foster a balanced understanding of identity and justice.

- **Promotion of Universal Principles:** Laws and social systems should be rooted in principles of equality, meritocracy, and fairness, rather than identity-based favoritism.

- **Empowerment Through Education:** Schools and universities must teach critical thinking and encourage open debate, enabling individuals to challenge ideological distortions.

- **Cultural Renewal:** Art, literature, and media should celebrate the diversity and complexity of human identity, rather than reinforcing divisive narratives.

Conclusion

The power of self-image on identity cannot be overstated. When manipulated, it becomes a devastating tool for alienating generations from their truth, fostering unjust hierarchies, and perpetuating systemic inequality. By understanding and addressing these distortions, society can work toward a future where identity is a source of strength and unity, rather than division and servitude.

CHAPTER 6: EXECUTIVE SINGULARITY

The concept of an executive singularity arises when a system or organization becomes self-contained, insular, and detached from the broader rule of law. This phenomenon prevents the executive function of the law—meant to ensure justice, safety, and equality—from serving the individuals entitled to its protection. Instead, these structures become mechanisms that prioritize internal procedures and ideologies over the universal application of rights, often resulting in systemic injustice.

This chapter examines the mechanisms by which executive singularities form, their impact on individuals within these systems, and the broader societal implications of such insular structures. Using examples like educational institutions shielding themselves from legal oversight, this chapter explores how these singularities undermine fundamental principles of justice and equality enshrined in the Universal Declaration of Human Rights (UDHR).

1. The Anatomy of an Executive Singularity

Executive singularities develop when systems or organizations prioritize their internal governance and ideological goals over external legal accountability.

- **Insularity:** Organizations create a self-referential framework where internal policies and procedures supersede external legal standards.

- **Exceptionalism:** These structures often justify their detachment from the rule of law by claiming a unique mission or purpose (e.g., protecting students or maintaining organizational autonomy).

- Bureaucratic Overreach: The complexity and rigidity of internal procedures make it nearly impossible for external intervention to occur, even when necessary to uphold justice.

Over time, these dynamics create a closed system where accountability to external legal and ethical standards is either diminished or entirely absent.

2. Case Study: Schools and the "Embassy" Mode

A clear example of an executive singularity can be found in certain educational systems where internal policies effectively shield institutions from external law enforcement.

- **Restricted Police Access:** In some school systems, incidents of violence, such as a student attacking a teacher, are handled exclusively through internal disciplinary measures, with police intervention discouraged or outright prohibited.

- **Impact on Teachers:** Teachers, as employees within these systems, are often stripped of their right to equal protection under the law. They are forced to rely on internal mechanisms that may prioritize the welfare of the student over the rights of the teacher.

- **Unequal Standards:** While individuals outside the institution enjoy full access to police protection, teachers within the system face diminished rights due to the singularity of the institution's governance.

This arrangement effectively creates a parallel legal system where certain individuals (e.g., teachers) are denied the full benefits of the law.

3. Impact on Human Rights and Justice

Executive singularities violate the principles of justice and equality established by the UDHR by creating environments where some individuals are systematically denied their rights.

- **Denial of Equal Protection:** Teachers in the aforementioned case are excluded from the protections afforded to every other citizen under the law.

- **Erosion of Personal Dignity:** By prioritizing the welfare of the offending party (e.g., the student) over the victim (e.g., the teacher), these systems devalue the dignity and humanity of those impacted by violence or injustice.

- **Systemic Injustice:** The lack of external oversight allows injustices to persist unchecked, eroding trust in the institution and the broader legal system.

When these singularities are allowed to proliferate, they create a fractured society where the rule of law is no longer universally applied.

4. Mechanisms of Perpetuation

Executive singularities are sustained by a combination of bureaucratic inertia, ideological entrenchment, and the absence of external accountability.

- **Bureaucratic Inertia:** The complexity of internal procedures discourages change and makes it difficult for individuals to seek redress outside the system.

- **Ideological Justification:** Organizations often frame their actions as being in service of a higher moral or ethical purpose, which insulates them from criticism.

- **Lack of Oversight:** Weak or absent mechanisms for external accountability allow these systems to operate independently of legal or ethical standards.

These factors create a self-reinforcing cycle where executive singularities become increasingly insulated and resistant to reform.

5. Broader Societal Implications

The existence of executive singularities within key institutions has far-reaching consequences for society at large.

- **Undermining the Rule of Law:** When certain groups or organizations operate outside the rule of law, it erodes the universality and fairness of legal protections.

- **Creation of Parallel Systems:** These singularities create fragmented systems of justice, where rights and protections vary depending on context or affiliation.

- **Normalization of Injustice:** Over time, the unequal application of the law becomes normalized, fostering a culture of impunity and systemic inequality.

If left unchecked, these dynamics can lead to widespread societal disintegration, as trust in legal and institutional frameworks erodes.

6. Restoring the Balance

To counteract the formation and impact of executive singularities, it is essential to restore the primacy of universal legal and ethical standards.

- **External Oversight:** Independent bodies must be empowered to monitor and enforce accountability within insular systems.

- **Legal Reform:** Laws must be updated to ensure that no organization can shield itself from external legal scrutiny.

- **Empowering Individuals:** Those within these systems must be given clear pathways to seek redress outside the organizational structure.

- **Cultural Change:** Society must reject the normalization of insularity and reaffirm its commitment to the principles of justice and equality.

By addressing these factors, it is possible to dismantle executive singularities and restore the universality of the rule of law.

Conclusion

Executive singularities represent a dangerous deviation from the principles of justice, equality, and accountability that underpin a functional society. By allowing certain organizations to operate as self-contained entities detached from the rule of law, these systems perpetuate systemic injustice and erode trust in legal and institutional frameworks. Recognizing and addressing the mechanisms that enable executive singularities is essential for creating a fair, just, and equitable society.

CHAPTER 7: EXECUTIVE LAW ENFORCEMENT OFFICERS

The phenomenon of Executive Singularity extends

to law enforcement when specific subsets of

officers or organizations become detached from

the broader legal framework governed by universal

principles, such as those outlined in the Universal Declaration of Human Rights (UDHR). Instead, these officers or units operate according to localized or organization-specific rules, creating disparities in how law is applied and justice is served. This chapter examines how this divergence manifests, using the example of community officers and their interactions with traditional police forces, and explores the consequences of such detachment from the broader rule of law.

1. Understanding the Executive Singularity in Law Enforcement

An executive singularity in law enforcement arises when:

1. **Subgroups** or specialized units operate under rules or guidelines that deviate from the universal standards of law enforcement.

2. **Their decisions**, despite being rooted in localized frameworks, are treated as equivalent to those made by officers operating under broader legal and regulatory standards.

3. **The entire law enforcement body** supports and reinforces such decisions, effectively institutionalizing this deviation.

This detachment creates a fractured system of law enforcement where the interpretation and execution of justice can vary significantly, undermining public trust and the principle of equality before the law.

2. Case Study: Community Officers vs. Police Officers

Community officers are often employed as a bridge between law enforcement and the communities they serve. However, their operational framework can differ significantly from that of traditional police officers:

- **Training and Authority:** Community officers may receive less comprehensive training than police officers and often have a narrower scope of authority.

- **Reporting and Accountability:** Their actions and decisions are sometimes governed by local organizational policies rather than the overarching legal standards applied to police officers.

- **Perceived Parity:** Despite these differences, their reports and executive decisions can carry the same legal weight as those of fully trained police officers, leading to potential discrepancies in the quality and fairness of law enforcement.

When the broader police department uncritically supports these decisions, it effectively transfers the authority of the entire department to a subgroup operating under a potentially flawed or limited framework.

3. The Risks of Divergent Frameworks

Allowing localized rules or organizational policies to dictate law enforcement actions creates several risks:

- **Inconsistent Application of Law:** Different groups within law enforcement may apply laws differently, leading to unequal treatment of individuals based on geography, identity, or other factors.

- **Erosion of Public Trust:** When citizens perceive that law enforcement operates under disparate standards, trust in the system diminishes.

- **Institutional Bias:** Organizations may impose rules or practices that reflect their own biases, which can then influence law enforcement decisions.

- **Unchecked Power:** If an entire police department supports the decisions of a subgroup without critical oversight, it creates a feedback loop that insulates the subgroup from accountability.

4. Institutional Backing and the Consolidation of Power

The issue becomes more pronounced when the broader law enforcement body unconditionally backs the decisions and actions of localized units or individuals. This institutional backing effectively consolidates power within the subgroup, granting it:

- **De Facto Authority:** The subgroup's decisions carry the weight of the entire department, even if they deviate from universal legal standards.

- **Immunity from Oversight:** Institutional support can shield the subgroup from external scrutiny, making it difficult to challenge or correct improper actions.

- **Expansion of Influence:** Over time, the practices and policies of the subgroup can influence the broader department, leading to systemic deviations from the rule of law.

This dynamic transforms the subgroup into a singularity within law enforcement, operating with a level of autonomy and authority that undermines the broader legal framework.

5. Broader Implications for Justice and Equality

The existence of executive singularities in law enforcement has profound implications for the justice system and society as a whole:

- **Undermining the Rule of Law:** When law enforcement operates under localized rules rather than universal legal standards, it creates a fragmented system where justice is applied inconsistently.

- **Exacerbation of Inequality:** Marginalized communities are often disproportionately affected by these discrepancies, further deepening societal divides.

- **Loss of Accountability:** Insular practices make it difficult to hold law enforcement accountable for misconduct or systemic failures.

These factors contribute to a breakdown in the social contract, as citizens lose faith in the ability of law enforcement to serve and protect impartially.

6. Restoring Accountability and Universal Standards

To address the challenges posed by executive singularities in law enforcement, it is essential to implement reforms that reinforce the primacy of universal legal and ethical standards.

- **Standardized Training and Protocols:** All law enforcement officers, regardless of their role or affiliation, should be trained to the same standard and operate under the same protocols.

- **Independent Oversight:** External bodies should be empowered to review and address discrepancies in law enforcement practices, ensuring accountability across all levels.

- **Clear Lines of Authority:** The roles and responsibilities of different law enforcement groups should be clearly defined, with mechanisms to ensure that decisions are made within the bounds of the law.

- **Public Transparency:** Law enforcement agencies should operate transparently, allowing citizens to understand and scrutinize their practices and decisions.

These measures can help to dismantle executive singularities and restore public confidence in the justice system.

Conclusion

The emergence of executive singularities within law enforcement represents a significant threat to the principles of justice, equality, and accountability. By allowing certain groups to operate under localized frameworks, insulated from external scrutiny, these singularities create a fractured system that undermines the rule of law. Recognizing and addressing these dynamics is essential for ensuring that law enforcement serves all citizens fairly and impartially, in line with the universal principles of the UDHR.

CHAPTER 8: EXECUTIVE SINGULARITY AND REDEFINITION OF REALITY

In the architecture of any society, the executive arm of governance—the point where laws, regulations, and constitutional ideals meet everyday implementation—is critical to shaping the lived reality of its people. While constitutions, legal frameworks, and declarations such as the Universal Declaration of Human Rights (UDHR) provide the blueprint for justice and equality, the actual experience of these principles is determined by how they are enforced. This chapter explores how the redefinition of key terms such as "privilege", "equity", "inclusion", "bias", and "underserved" can create an "Executive Singularity", effectively transforming the application of laws and reshaping societal reality.

Through these redefinitions, the executive function of law enforcement and governance can shift away from universality and impartiality, creating a new social hierarchy where justice, fairness, and protection become privileges reserved for select groups. This phenomenon reveals that the "lived reality" of justice is not determined by the ideals enshrined in constitutions but by how they are executed on a daily basis.

1. The Power of Words in Shaping Reality

Language is not only a tool for communication but also a framework for understanding and shaping reality. Words like "privilege", "equity", "inclusion", and "bias" carry immense ideological weight. When these terms are redefined, they can:

- Change the interpretation of laws.

- Influence the priorities of law enforcement and governance.

- Create new social norms that affect the distribution of resources and justice.

For example:

- **Privilege:** Traditionally understood as an unearned advantage, this term can be redefined to justify systemic redistribution of rights, protections, and resources in a way that creates new hierarchies.

- **Equity:** While equality aims for impartial treatment, equity—redefined as equal outcomes—can lead to selective application of laws and services.

- **Inclusion:** This term, reframed as prioritizing specific groups, can lead to policies that exclude or marginalize others under the guise of inclusion.

- **Bias:** Expanded interpretations can justify intrusive policies that disproportionately affect certain groups while excusing others.

These redefinitions reshape the operational priorities of executive systems, changing the way justice is applied and resources are distributed.

2. The Role of Law Enforcement in Defining Reality

Law enforcement is the bridge between abstract legal frameworks and the lived experience of justice. The execution of the law determines whether:

- People feel safe in their communities.
- Their rights are upheld in practice.
- They perceive fairness and impartiality in their interactions with authority.

When law enforcement operates under redefined terms, the outcome is a selective application of justice, creating disparities in the protection and service individuals receive. This selective application can:

1. Prioritize One Group Over Another: By redefining terms like "privilege" and *underserved*, certain groups may be given preferential treatment at the expense of others.

2. Redefine Victimhood: The designation of who is considered a victim becomes fluid, often dictated by political or ideological agendas.

3. Transform Policing Priorities: Law enforcement may focus on enforcing policies aligned with new definitions rather than addressing universal safety and justice concerns.

---

3. Selective Justice and Everyday Reality

The real impact of this phenomenon is felt in the daily lives of individuals. For example:

- **Crime Response:** Certain neighborhoods or demographics may experience delayed or inadequate law enforcement response due to re-prioritized resource allocation based on equity goals.

- **Legal Protections:** Groups deemed "privileged" may face reduced protections under the law, while those considered "underserved" receive heightened protections.

- **Judicial Outcomes:** Court decisions can increasingly reflect ideological interpretations of equity and inclusion rather than impartial legal reasoning.

The result is a stratified society where justice and protection are no longer universally accessible but are contingent on identity, status, or alignment with redefined terms.

4. The International Perspective on Rule of Law

Globally, the rule of law is a cornerstone for measuring a country's development and governance quality. Indicators include:

- **Democratic Institutions:** Transparent and accountable systems of governance.

- **Fair Legal Practices:** Equal treatment under the law.

- **Crime Rates and Policing:** Effective and impartial enforcement of laws.

Countries are judged not by the laws they "declare" but by how those laws are "executed". For example:

- A nation with a comprehensive constitution but selective law enforcement will be considered less developed.

- Conversely, a society where law enforcement upholds universal principles of justice and equality is seen as advanced, even if its legal framework is less comprehensive on paper.

This discrepancy underscores the importance of the executive arm of governance in shaping the reality of the rule of law.

5. The Determinism of Redefinition

The redefinition of key terms creates a feedback loop that solidifies a new social reality:

1. Ideological Justification: Redefinitions provide the ideological foundation for policy changes.

2. Institutional Implementation: These policies are embedded within law enforcement and governance systems.

3. Daily Reinforcement: The selective application of laws reinforces the new social order, making it the lived reality for citizens.

4. Normalization: Over time, these practices become accepted as the *natural* or *correct* way of operating.

For those living under this system, the result is a deterministic reality shaped by a few altered definitions, regardless of the ideals enshrined in constitutional or legal documents.

6. Conclusion: Redefinition as Reality Determinism

The power of redefinition lies in its ability to reshape the execution of laws, which in turn determines the lived reality of justice, equality, and protection. While constitutions and the UDHR may remain unchanged on paper, their practical significance is diminished when the executive arm of governance operates under localized, ideologically driven frameworks.

This phenomenon highlights the fragility of the rule of law and the profound impact of language on governance. A society's reality is not defined by the ideals it proclaims but by the daily actions of its institutions. When words like "equity", "privilege", and "bias" are redefined to serve specific agendas, they have the power to alter the structure of justice itself, creating a new hierarchy of privilege and protection.

Ultimately, the redefinition of key terms acts as a form of determinism, locking societies into a new reality dictated by the selective application of laws and the prioritization of specific groups. Recognizing and addressing this dynamic is essential for preserving the universality and impartiality of justice in any society.

CHAPTER 9: SCHOOL BOARDS EXECUTIVE SINGULARITY AND HR CODE

Introduction

School boards play a crucial role in shaping the educational environment and ensuring that schools are safe, inclusive spaces. In recent years, many boards have taken significant steps to address issues related to Human Rights Code (HR Code) protected grounds, such as bullying, discrimination, and fostering equity. However, in doing so, some boards have become insular in their approach, effectively operating in a form of "embassy mode."

This chapter examines how school boards' discretionary application of HR Code principles can lead to an Executive Singularity—a condition where their practices become isolated from broader societal consensus, public regulation, and legal frameworks. While well-intentioned, this isolation can undermine universal protections and create inconsistencies in how rights are upheld and exercised.

1. "Embassy Mode" in School Boards

The term "embassy mode" is used here to describe how school boards operate as insulated entities, exercising significant autonomy in defining and enforcing HR Code-related policies. This includes:

- **Internal Authority:** Boards often create and enforce policies that go beyond ministry or governmental directives, asserting their discretion in how HR Code principles are applied.

- Closed Decision-Making: Issues of discrimination, equity, and inclusion are handled internally, often without external scrutiny or accountability.

- Policy Imposition: Boards sometimes claim their internal practices are best suited for broader implementation, pressuring ministries and governments to adopt their approaches.

For example, a school board might develop specific protocols to address bullying or harassment related to HR Code-protected grounds, yet these protocols may not align with broader societal standards or legal norms.

2. Implications of Insular Practices

The insulated nature of some school boards' practices has far-reaching implications, including:

1. Inconsistent Rights Protections: Students and staff within schools may experience different levels of rights protection compared to those in broader society.

2. Lack of Public Oversight: Boards operate with limited input from the public or other stakeholders, leading to potential biases in how policies are developed and enforced.

3. Reduced Transparency: Decisions regarding sensitive issues are often made behind closed doors, with little accountability to affected communities or external bodies.

4. Fragmented Justice: The application of HR Code principles may vary significantly from one board to another, creating disparities in how rights are understood and exercised.

3. Challenges of Isolated Enforcement

While school boards often present themselves as champions of equity and inclusion, their insular enforcement of HR Code principles can create unintended challenges:

- **Lack of Consistency:** Without standardized guidelines, policies differ across schools and boards, leading to uneven outcomes for students and staff.

- **Perceived Partiality:** In focusing on certain protected grounds, boards may inadvertently neglect other aspects of equity and inclusion, creating a perception of bias.

- **Internal Limitations:** Boards may lack the expertise, resources, or legal authority to address complex issues effectively, leading to superficial or inconsistent enforcement.

For example, students experiencing harassment may find that their school's internal processes are insufficient or unevenly applied, yet they are discouraged from seeking external support due to the board's self-contained approach.

4. The Need for Standardized Oversight

Addressing issues of equity and inclusion requires a coordinated, society-wide effort. This effort should include:

1. Uniform Policies: National or regional standards for addressing HR Code-protected grounds should be established to ensure consistency across all schools and boards.

2. Collaborative Decision-Making: Policies should be developed with input from diverse stakeholders, including students, parents, educators, and community organizations.

3. Enhanced Transparency: School boards must operate with greater openness, allowing for public scrutiny and accountability.

4. Alignment with Broader Society: Internal policies should complement, rather than replace, societal standards and legal frameworks for equity and inclusion.

5. Balancing Rights and Responsibilities

Effective equity and inclusion policies must balance the rights and responsibilities of all individuals involved. This includes:

- Ensuring that students and staff are treated fairly and respectfully, regardless of their backgrounds or identities.

- Recognizing that schools are part of a larger societal framework and must align their policies with public laws and standards.

- Addressing issues holistically, without prioritizing certain protected grounds over others, to foster a truly inclusive environment.

6. Moving Toward Inclusive Integration

To overcome the challenges of Executive Singularity in school boards, it is essential to adopt a more integrated approach to equity and inclusion. Key steps include:

1. Unified Standards: Establishing clear, consistent guidelines for addressing HR Code-protected grounds across all schools and boards.

2. Collaborative Efforts: Encouraging cooperation between school boards, governments, and community organizations to develop and implement policies.

3. Transparent Practices: Ensuring that all decisions related to equity and inclusion are made openly and with input from affected stakeholders.

4. Ongoing Education: Providing training and resources to educators, administrators, and students to foster understanding and respect for all protected grounds.

Conclusion

The insular practices of some school boards, while often well-meaning, risk creating a fragmented approach to equity and inclusion that undermines the universal protections guaranteed by law. By operating in "embassy mode," boards isolate themselves from the larger societal frameworks meant to uphold and protect human rights.

To address these challenges, society must work toward a unified, transparent, and inclusive framework for equity and inclusion that ensures consistency, accountability, and fairness for all. Only by integrating school policies with broader societal standards can we create an environment that truly serves and respects the rights of every individual.

CHAPTER 10: SUBVERSION OF DECISION-MAKING HIERARCHY

Introduction

The integrity of a legal system hinges on the separation of powers and the impartial execution of the law. When an institution manipulates the executive function of the law to serve its own interests, it disrupts this balance, creating a Subversion of Decision-Making Hierarchy. This phenomenon occurs when an institution not only hijacks the law's executive function but also redefines the processes of lawmaking and enforcement to justify its ongoing transgressions.

This chapter examines the devastating effects of such subversion, exploring how the law's executive function is distorted, the broader implications for justice and governance, and the systemic risks of allowing executive bodies to dictate policy as a means of self-preservation.

1. Hijacking the Executive Function of the Law

The executive function of the law ensures that decisions made by legislative and judicial bodies are carried out fairly and impartially. When this function is co-opted by a local group, organization, or ideology, the law ceases to serve its universal purpose. Instead, it becomes a tool for advancing the interests of those in control.

- **Localized Control:** Institutions bypass broader legal frameworks, executing laws based on internal policies or ideological agendas.

- **Selective Justice:** The law is applied unequally, benefiting specific groups while neglecting or actively harming others.

- **Creation of Loopholes:** Executive actions are justified retroactively, often through manufactured legal loopholes or reinterpretations of existing laws.

For instance, an institution that operates under the guise of equity may prioritize its favored ideology or group, enforcing rules selectively while excluding others from the same protections.

2. Justice Denied: Unequal Application of the Law

When the executive function is hijacked, justice becomes fragmented and inaccessible. Key consequences include:

- **Systemic Bias:** Certain individuals or groups are systematically excluded from fair treatment under the law.

- **Legal Limbo:** Those affected by the subversion may find themselves without recourse, as the institution shields itself from external accountability.

- Loss of Public Trust: A legal system perceived as biased erodes public confidence, weakening societal cohesion and respect for the rule of law.

Example: In some cases, internal protocols within institutions override external legal standards, leaving individuals who should be protected by the law without adequate recourse.

3. Institutional Overreach: Dictating Policy to Policymakers

A particularly dangerous outcome of executive subversion is the reversal of the traditional hierarchy of governance. Instead of being guided by legislative frameworks, the institution begins dictating policy to policymakers.

- **Reactive Policymaking:** Legislators are pressured to codify the institution's internal practices into law, often without broader societal input.

- **Exoneration Mechanisms:** New policies are crafted to retroactively absolve the institution of responsibility for past transgressions.

- **Self-Perpetuation:** The institution entrenches its practices, creating a cycle where its decisions become the basis for future lawmaking.

This shift undermines democratic processes, as laws are no longer created through collective deliberation but are instead dictated by entities with vested interests.

4. Subversion of Legal Decision-Making

In a functioning legal system, decisions are made through transparent, accountable processes. Subversion occurs when the executive body not only executes the law selectively but also manipulates the decision-making process itself.

- **Preemptive Justifications:** Policies are designed to rationalize decisions that have already been made, regardless of legality or fairness.

- **Criminal Actions Legitimized:** Ongoing transgressions are reframed as necessary or inevitable, often under the guise of addressing systemic issues.

- **Policy as a Shield:** Legal frameworks are distorted to protect the institution from scrutiny, rather than ensuring justice.

Example: An organization accused of wrongdoing might lobby for changes in the law that redefine its actions as permissible, effectively absolving itself of liability.

5. Law as a Justification for Crime

When subversion reaches its peak, the law itself becomes a tool for justifying ongoing transgressions. This creates a paradoxical situation where criminal actions are both committed and legitimized under the guise of legality.

- **Erosion of Accountability:** The perpetrators of injustice operate with impunity, shielded by the very laws they manipulate.

- **Institutionalized Corruption:** The legal system becomes complicit in wrongdoing, undermining its credibility and effectiveness.

- **Normalization of Injustice:** Over time, these practices become accepted as the norm, further entrenching systemic inequality.

6. Truncation of Governance

As the executive body gains dominance, the broader structure of governance is weakened. Key impacts include:

- **Reduced Oversight:** Legislative and judicial bodies are sidelined, limiting their ability to hold the executive accountable.

- **Centralized Power:** Decision-making becomes concentrated in the hands of a few, bypassing checks and balances.

- **Stagnation of Reform:** The system becomes resistant to change, perpetuating injustice and inefficiency.

Example: A police department that consistently shields its officers from accountability may effectively operate as an autonomous entity, undermining public trust in law enforcement and governance.

7. The Executive as Law-Maker and Decision-Maker

When the executive body assumes the roles of both lawmaker and decision-maker, it becomes a de facto authority, answerable only to itself. This consolidation of power is inherently dangerous:

- **Conflict of Interest:** The same entity that enforces the law also determines its content, eliminating impartiality.

- **Perpetual Exoneration:** By controlling both lawmaking and enforcement, the body ensures that its actions are never subject to meaningful scrutiny.

- **Loss of Justice:** The legal system becomes a façade, serving the interests of the powerful rather than upholding universal principles of fairness.

Conclusion

The subversion of decision-making hierarchy represents a profound threat to justice, governance, and the rule of law. When institutions manipulate the executive function to serve their own interests, they distort the balance of power, undermine public trust, and perpetuate systemic injustice.

To prevent such subversion, it is essential to strengthen oversight mechanisms, ensure the separation of powers, and uphold the universal application of the law. Only by addressing these challenges can we restore the integrity of our legal systems and ensure that justice is truly served.

CHAPTER 11: GOVERNANCE SINGULARITY

Introduction

The concept of a Governance Singularity emerges when localized institutions, initially designed to serve specific functions, expand their authority to the extent that they redefine governance itself. When the executive body of the law is subverted and hierarchies are distorted, the cumulative effect cascades across the entire structure of government. The result is that localized institutions—whether school boards, police departments, regulatory agencies, or other organizations—become the de facto rulers, dictating not just policy but the daily reality of life for all citizens.

In this chapter, we analyze how the erosion of hierarchical governance leads to the centralization of power within localized institutions. This shift causes a complete breakdown in the separation of powers, creating a scenario where a single institution or group acts as judge, jury, executioner, and law enforcement officer. The implications of this phenomenon are explored through its effects on society, governance, and the rule of law.

1. Localized Institutions as Governance Entities

Localized institutions are designed to operate within the broader framework of government, implementing policies and laws as directed by higher authorities. However, when these institutions subvert the executive function, they begin to transcend their original roles.

- **Expansion of Authority:** These institutions extend their reach beyond their initial mandate, making decisions that should reside at the governmental or judicial level.

- **Interpretation as Power:** By interpreting laws and policies to suit their interests, they effectively rewrite the rules of governance within their sphere of influence.

- **Creation of Autonomous Ecosystems:** Over time, these entities develop internal mechanisms of governance that operate independently of the state.

For example, a school board that enforces its own policies in ways that override legal statutes is no longer merely an administrative body; it becomes a governing entity within its jurisdiction.

2. Subversion of Hierarchical Governance

The hierarchical structure of governance exists to ensure accountability and balance. When local institutions undermine this structure, they weaken the broader system of checks and balances.

- **Erosion of Oversight:** Higher authorities, such as legislatures or courts, lose their ability to monitor and regulate the actions of localized institutions.

- **Usurpation of Power:** Decisions that should involve broader societal deliberation are made unilaterally by localized bodies.

- **Inversion of Authority:** Instead of being accountable to the government, these institutions begin to hold the government accountable to their own rules and interpretations.

For example, a regulatory agency that enforces policies contradicting national laws might compel lawmakers to adapt legislation to align with its actions, effectively dictating policy at the national level.

3. Daily Reality as Dictated by Localized Institutions

The governance singularity becomes most apparent in the daily lives of citizens. The interpretation and execution of laws by localized institutions create a lived reality that often contradicts the broader principles of governance.

- **Fragmented Justice:** Citizens experience different standards of justice depending on the institution governing their specific context.

- **Selective Enforcement:** Localized institutions prioritize their interests, enforcing laws in ways that benefit certain groups while neglecting others.

- **Normalization of Power Asymmetry:** Over time, the public comes to accept the dominance of these institutions as a normal aspect of governance.

Example: In a jurisdiction where police departments operate autonomously, citizens might face vastly different treatment based on the specific policies of their local precinct rather than national laws.

4. Localized Institutions as Judge, Jury, and Executioner

A key feature of the governance singularity is the concentration of power within localized institutions, allowing them to assume multiple roles traditionally separated within a functioning government.

- **Judicial Role:** These institutions interpret laws and policies to justify their actions, effectively acting as judges within their domain.

- **Legislative Role:** By creating internal rules and policies, they legislate without oversight or accountability.

- **Executive Role:** They enforce these rules with little regard for external standards or constraints.

This consolidation of power creates a closed system where accountability is nonexistent, and the rule of law is replaced by the rule of the institution.

5. Government Held Hostage

As localized institutions gain power, they begin to dictate terms to the broader government. This dynamic effectively holds the government hostage, forcing it to align with the institution's agenda.

- **Policy Capture:** Legislators and policymakers are pressured to codify the institution's practices into law, often under the guise of efficiency or expertise.

- **Resource Diversion:** Government resources are redirected to support the institution's priorities, often at the expense of broader societal needs.

- **Immunity from Scrutiny:** These institutions shield themselves from accountability by controlling the narrative and legal framework surrounding their actions.

Example: A city council dominated by a single interest group might implement policies that prioritize that group's agenda, compelling state or national governments to adapt their policies accordingly.

6. Consequences for Democracy and the Rule of Law

The governance singularity has profound implications for democracy and the rule of law. By concentrating power within localized institutions, it undermines the principles of fairness, equality, and accountability.

- **Democratic Erosion:** The concentration of power within unelected bodies diminishes the influence of democratic processes.

- **Legal Fragmentation:** The law becomes inconsistent and unpredictable, varying widely based on the jurisdiction or institution in control.

- **Loss of Public Trust:** Citizens lose faith in governance, perceiving it as a tool for advancing the interests of the powerful rather than serving the public good.

7. Breaking the Cycle of Governance Singularity

Addressing the governance singularity requires a concerted effort to restore balance and accountability within the system. Key strategies include:

- **Strengthening Oversight:** Establishing robust mechanisms to monitor and regulate the actions of localized institutions.

- **Reaffirming Hierarchical Governance:** Ensuring that localized bodies operate within the framework of national laws and policies.

- **Promoting Transparency:** Mandating clear and open decision-making processes to prevent the concentration of power.

Conclusion

The governance singularity represents a critical threat to the integrity of democratic institutions and the rule of law. By allowing localized institutions to dictate governance, we risk creating a fragmented and inequitable society where justice and accountability are subservient to the interests of the powerful.

Reversing this trend requires a renewed commitment to the principles of hierarchical governance, ensuring that power is exercised in the service of all citizens rather than the narrow interests of a few. Only by addressing this challenge can we safeguard the future of governance and uphold the ideals of democracy and justice.

CHAPTER 12: SINGULARITY OF AUTHORITY FIGURES

Introduction

Authority is often entrusted to individuals based on merit, experience, and the ability to lead and inspire others. However, when individuals lacking the essential traits of effective leadership—such as charisma, competence, vision, or the ability to mobilize people for positive change—ascend to positions of power, the consequences can be devastating. These leaders, aware of their deficiencies, often resort to monopolizing authority, centralizing control, and employing oppressive tactics to maintain their position. This phenomenon, which we term the Singularity of Authority Figures, reveals the dangers of placing power in the hands of those unqualified to wield it responsibly.

In this chapter, we will explore the dynamics of this singularity, examining the motivations, behaviors, and impacts of ineffective leaders in positions of authority. By analyzing historical and contemporary examples, we aim to illuminate the patterns of oppression, stagnation, and societal harm that emerge from such leadership.

1. The Roots of Ineffective Leadership

The ascension of individuals without the skills or character for leadership often stems from systemic flaws in governance, institutional practices, or societal norms. Key factors include:

- **Nepotism and Cronyism:** Leadership roles are given to individuals based on personal connections rather than merit.

- **Misplaced Priorities:** Selection processes prioritize loyalty, conformity, or ideology over competence and vision.

- **Institutional Rigidity:** Systems that fail to adapt or evolve may perpetuate the promotion of mediocrity.

- **Symbolic Representation:** Leaders are chosen to fulfill a symbolic or superficial criterion, such as identity or background, without regard for their ability to govern effectively.

These factors often result in leaders who lack the qualities necessary to inspire trust, mobilize support, or implement meaningful change.

2. Compensating for Deficiencies: The Mechanics of Control

When leaders recognize their inadequacies, they often resort to mechanisms of control and domination to compensate. These include:

- **Monopolization of Power:** Centralizing authority and reducing checks and balances to shield themselves from scrutiny.

- **Use of Fear and Coercion:** Employing intimidation, violence, or other oppressive tactics to suppress dissent and maintain order.

- **Bureaucratic Overreach:** Expanding bureaucratic control to micromanage every aspect of governance, stifling creativity and initiative.

- **Symbolic Displays of Authority:** Using rituals, propaganda, or grandiose projects to project an image of strength and capability.

This approach creates a feedback loop, as the leader's reliance on control further alienates and disempowers others, deepening the singularity of authority.

3. The Psychology of Ineffective Leaders

The actions of ineffective leaders are often driven by deep-seated insecurities and fears, which shape their behavior and decision-making.

- **Fear of Exposure:** A constant anxiety about being unmasked as incompetent drives excessive control and paranoia.

- **Need for Validation:** Insecure leaders seek constant affirmation, surrounding themselves with sycophants and suppressing dissent.

- **Overcompensation:** Leaders may adopt extreme or authoritarian policies to demonstrate strength, masking their weaknesses.

- **Resentment of Criticism:** Incompetent leaders often perceive criticism as a personal attack, leading to punitive actions against perceived adversaries.

These psychological dynamics not only harm governance but also create a toxic environment for those who work under such leaders.

4. Consequences of the Singularity of Authority Figures

The societal and organizational impacts of ineffective leadership are profound and far-reaching:

- **Erosion of Trust:** Public confidence in leadership and institutions declines, leading to widespread cynicism and disengagement.

- **Stifling of Innovation:** Centralized control discourages creativity, adaptability, and initiative, resulting in stagnation.

- **Perpetuation of Inequality:** Ineffective leaders often prioritize self-preservation over justice, perpetuating systemic inequalities.

- **Cycle of Oppression:** The oppressive tactics used to maintain power become entrenched, normalizing authoritarianism and violence.

- **Institutional Decay:** Over time, the concentration of power and lack of accountability weaken the structures of governance and administration.

These outcomes not only harm individuals and communities but also undermine the long-term stability and progress of societies.

5. Historical and Contemporary Examples

Throughout history, the singularity of authority figures has manifested in various forms, from despotic rulers to ineffectual administrators.

- **Despots and Dictators:** Leaders like Nero of Rome or Pol Pot of Cambodia relied on fear and violence to maintain power, compensating for their inability to govern effectively.

- **Corporate Mismanagement:** CEOs promoted for loyalty rather than competence have driven companies into decline through poor decision-making and authoritarian practices.

- **Bureaucratic Authoritarianism:** In some regimes, mid-level bureaucrats ascend to positions of power, stifling progress through excessive control and lack of vision.

These examples highlight the recurring patterns of harm and stagnation associated with ineffective leadership.

6. Breaking the Singularity

Addressing the singularity of authority figures requires systemic change at both the institutional and societal levels. Key strategies include:

- **Merit-Based Leadership:** Prioritizing competence, vision, and character in the selection and promotion of leaders.

- **Strengthening Accountability:** Implementing robust mechanisms to monitor and evaluate leadership performance.

- **Empowering Subordinates:** Encouraging initiative and participation at all levels to counterbalance centralized control.

- **Fostering a Culture of Learning:** Promoting humility, adaptability, and continuous self-improvement among leaders.

- **Public Engagement:** Ensuring that leadership is responsive to the needs and aspirations of the broader community.

By adopting these strategies, organizations and societies can mitigate the risks associated with ineffective leadership and promote more equitable and effective governance.

Conclusion

The singularity of authority figures represents a fundamental challenge to the principles of effective governance and social progress. When power is concentrated in the hands of those lacking the skills and character to wield it responsibly, the consequences ripple across society, undermining trust, innovation, and justice.

To overcome this challenge, we must confront the systemic flaws that enable ineffective leaders to ascend to power and create environments that support and reward true leadership. Only by addressing these issues can we build a future where authority is exercised with competence, integrity, and a genuine commitment to the greater good.

CHAPTER 13: CHANGE SINGULARITY

Introduction

Change is the lifeblood of societal progress and the foundation of any civilization striving to meet the ideals of justice, equality, and the Universal

Declaration of Human Rights (UDHR). Yet, when the sum of singularities—Executive, Governance, Authority Figures, and others—becomes entrenched, it creates a Change Singularity: a condition where a society fragments into isolated factions, each locked into its own internal logic and self-reinforcing mechanisms. In this state, the system's components cease to work collaboratively toward the greater good, stifling the ability to enact meaningful change and address systemic issues.

This chapter explores how such singularities arise, their impact on society's capacity for collective action, and the mechanisms that trap societies in cycles of stagnation and fragmentation. Through analysis and examples, we reveal the far-reaching consequences of this phenomenon and propose pathways to break free from the inertia of the Change Singularity.

1. The Anatomy of Change Singularity

At its core, the Change Singularity emerges when institutions, organizations, and social systems operate in silos, disconnected from the broader goals of societal advancement. The following dynamics contribute to its formation:

- **Fragmentation of Purpose:** Different sectors—education, law enforcement, governance, and civil society—pursue their own interests, often at odds with the collective good.

- **Closed Loops of Decision-Making:** Institutions become self-referential, making decisions based on internal priorities rather than societal needs.

- **Conflict of Interest:** Competing ideologies, power struggles, and vested interests prevent collaboration and consensus-building.

- **Entrenchment of Singularities:** Each singularity (e.g., Executive, Governance, or Authority Figures) reinforces its own existence, creating barriers to change and coordination.

These dynamics lead to a fractured society where progress is not only slowed but actively obstructed by the very structures meant to facilitate it.

2. The Effects of Fragmentation on Society

The fragmentation caused by the Change Singularity manifests in several ways:

- **Policy Paralysis:** With no unified vision or cooperative effort, policies addressing critical societal issues become disjointed, ineffective, or contradictory.

- **Social Inequity:** Resources and protections are unevenly distributed, benefiting some groups while marginalizing others.

- **Loss of Public Trust:** People lose faith in institutions that fail to deliver justice, equality, or progress, leading to disengagement and apathy.

- **Stagnation of Innovation:** Silos and isolated systems stifle creativity and cross-sector collaboration, hindering advancements in science, technology, and culture.

This fragmentation creates a vicious cycle: as societal cohesion weakens, the ability to enact meaningful change diminishes further, deepening the Change Singularity.

3. Mechanisms That Perpetuate Change Singularity

Several mechanisms lock societies into the Change Singularity:

- **Institutional Self-Preservation:** Institutions prioritize their survival and autonomy over collaboration, often resisting external input or reform.

- **Ideological Entrenchment:** Competing ideologies create rigid boundaries that prevent compromise or shared action.

- **Legal and Procedural Barriers:** Overly complex or contradictory laws and procedures hinder coordinated efforts and make systemic reform nearly impossible.

- **Mistrust and Polarization:** Lack of trust between groups—whether governmental, social, or institutional—further isolates them and prevents collaboration.

These mechanisms not only sustain the singularity but also amplify its effects over time, making it increasingly difficult to break free.

4. The Inertia of Change Singularity in Practice

The real-world impact of Change Singularity can be seen in various societal failures:

- **Healthcare Inequities:** Disconnected healthcare systems fail to provide universal access, leaving some populations underserved while others receive disproportionate resources.

- **Educational Disparities:** Fragmented school systems create unequal opportunities, perpetuating cycles of poverty and privilege.

- Justice System Failures: Singularities within law enforcement and governance create selective justice, undermining the rule of law.

- Climate Inaction: Competing interests and fragmented approaches prevent effective action on global issues like climate change.

These examples illustrate how the Change Singularity manifests in diverse contexts, locking societies into patterns of inequality, inefficiency, and stagnation.

5. Breaking Free: Pathways to Overcome Change Singularity

Addressing the Change Singularity requires systemic change and collective effort. Key strategies include:

1. Fostering Interconnection

- Establish mechanisms for cross-sector collaboration, ensuring that institutions and organizations work together toward shared goals.

- Create platforms for dialogue and cooperation that bridge ideological divides and promote mutual understanding.

2. Simplifying and Unifying Legal Frameworks

- Streamline laws and procedures to reduce complexity and contradictions that hinder coordination.

- Ensure that all institutions operate under a common legal and ethical framework aligned with the UDHR.

3. Rebuilding Trust

- Promote transparency and accountability in governance and decision-making to restore public faith in institutions.

- Encourage participatory approaches that involve citizens in shaping policies and reforms.

4. Prioritizing Equity and Inclusion

- Address systemic inequities by ensuring that all groups have access to resources, protections, and opportunities.

- Challenge entrenched power structures that perpetuate privilege and marginalization.

5. Empowering Visionary Leadership

- Promote leaders who possess the charisma, competence, and vision to inspire collective action and drive meaningful change.

- Develop leadership programs that emphasize collaboration, adaptability, and a commitment to the greater good.

6. A Vision for the Future

Breaking free from the Change Singularity requires more than systemic reform; it demands a fundamental shift in societal values and priorities. Societies must embrace:

- **A Shared Commitment to the Greater Good:** Recognizing that the well-being of one group is intrinsically tied to the well-being of all.

- **A Culture of Adaptation and Resilience:** Fostering flexibility and innovation to address emerging challenges and opportunities.

- **A Focus on Universal Human Rights:** Ensuring that the principles of the UDHR are not just ideals but lived realities for all.

By adopting these principles, societies can move beyond the inertia of the Change Singularity, creating systems and structures that support sustainable progress and the advancement of civilization.

Conclusion

The Change Singularity represents a profound challenge to the ideals of justice, equality, and progress. When societies fragment into isolated singularities, they lose the ability to work together, innovate, and address the needs of their people.

However, this challenge also presents an opportunity: to confront the systemic flaws that sustain the singularity and to build a future based on collaboration, equity, and shared purpose. By breaking free from the loops of stagnation and fragmentation, societies can unlock their potential and fulfill the promise of the UDHR, advancing toward a more just and unified world.

CHAPTER 14: THE ANTI-CHANGE SINGULARITY

The "Anti-Change Singularity" represents a critical and destabilizing phenomenon within modern governance and societal structures. It emerges when individuals or groups strategically position themselves within key institutions of power and authority, not to serve the public good but to advance the agenda of a network or ideology they are loyal to. These individuals, instead of adhering to their formal job descriptions and responsibilities, become extensions of these networks, effectively creating small, self-contained "kingdoms" or "pirate islands" that operate outside the broader rule of law.

The Formation of Anti-Change Networks

At the heart of the Anti-Change Singularity lies a network of individuals united by shared interests, ideologies, or criminal motivations. These networks infiltrate positions of influence within public services, governance, or enforcement bodies. Their members prioritize the directives and objectives of their network over the duties prescribed by their official roles.

For instance:

1. Public Services as Tools of Control: In health care, education, or housing, decisions that directly impact the quality of life for citizens are filtered through the lens of the network's goals. Instead of equitable distribution of resources or justice, the network ensures benefits flow disproportionately to its own members or allies.

2. Judicial Manipulation: Within law enforcement or judicial systems, these networks ensure selective application of the law. Certain individuals or groups are shielded from accountability, while others are disproportionately targeted.

3. Administrative Gatekeeping: Bureaucrats loyal to the network create barriers to access essential services for those outside their circle while fast-tracking benefits for their own.

Hierarchy Within the "Kingdoms"

These networks function like autonomous entities, complete with their own hierarchies, codes of conduct, and internal rules:

- **Commanders-in-Chief:** At the top of the pyramid are individuals who act as decision-makers. They issue directives to the lower tiers of the network, often overriding or subverting official protocols.

- **Enforcers:** Mid-level members ensure compliance within the network, leveraging both incentives and punishments to maintain loyalty.

- **Foot Soldiers:** These are the operatives embedded within institutions, executing the orders of their commanders, often under the guise of performing their public duties.

This structure creates an impenetrable system where decisions are not based on merit, legality, or public need but are dictated by the internal goals of the network.

The Consequences of Anti-Change Singularities

1. Undermining Rule of Law: The authority of legal and constitutional frameworks is diminished as these networks prioritize their own rules and directives.

2. Erosion of Public Trust: Citizens lose faith in institutions meant to serve them, perceiving them as biased, corrupt, or ineffective.

3. Systemic Inequality: Resources, justice, and opportunities are unfairly distributed, exacerbating societal divides.

4. Resistance to Change: These networks actively block reforms or initiatives that threaten their autonomy or interests, stalling societal progress.

Real-World Examples

- **Educational Systems:** In some school boards, policies and decisions are made based on ideological loyalties rather than the best interests of students. These boards operate as closed entities, resistant to external scrutiny or accountability.

- **Healthcare Systems:** Access to medical care can be skewed by administrators who prioritize members of their network or ideology, leaving others underserved.

- **Local Governments:** In municipalities, zoning laws, public works projects, or housing policies are manipulated to favor specific groups, creating pockets of privilege amidst widespread neglect.

The Pirate-Island Phenomenon

The analogy of a "pirate island" aptly describes these networks. Much like a pirate crew that follows its own code, these groups operate with their own internal governance, rejecting oversight or accountability to external authorities. These islands are fortified by:

1. Insularity: Members are loyal to the network, protecting it from external interference.

2. Self-Sufficiency: The network creates self-sustaining systems, ensuring its survival and autonomy.

3. Expansionist Tendencies: As the network grows, it seeks to infiltrate more areas of public life, increasing its influence and control.

Interference with Change and Progress

The Anti-Change Singularity thrives on resisting any effort that threatens its dominance or disrupts its operations:

- **Blocking Reforms:** Legislative changes or policy reforms that aim to increase transparency or accountability are met with intense resistance.

- **Rewriting Narratives:** The network controls information to shape public perception, ensuring its actions are seen as legitimate or necessary.

- **Sabotaging Opponents:** Whistleblowers or reformers within institutions are marginalized, discredited, or removed.

Solutions to the Anti-Change Singularity

Addressing this phenomenon requires a multi-faceted approach:

1. Strengthening Oversight: Independent bodies must monitor institutions to ensure adherence to legal and ethical standards.

2. Promoting Transparency: Decisions and actions within public services must be open to scrutiny to prevent undue influence.

3. Encouraging Whistleblowing: Protections and incentives for whistleblowers can expose and dismantle these networks.

4. Fostering Public Awareness: Educating citizens about the existence and impact of such networks can galvanize demand for accountability and reform.

5. Legislative Reforms: Laws must be enacted to close loopholes that allow these networks to flourish.

Conclusion

The Anti-Change Singularity represents a grave threat to the integrity of institutions, the rule of law, and the progress of society. By creating self-contained "kingdoms" within the broader system, these networks disrupt the delivery of justice, equality, and public service. Recognizing and addressing this phenomenon is essential to ensuring that institutions remain accountable, transparent, and dedicated to serving the greater good rather than the narrow interests of a select few. The fight against the Anti-Change Singularity is, ultimately, a fight for the soul of governance and the future of society.

CONCLUSION

In tracing the intricate web of social agency singularities throughout this book, we have uncovered a profound and pervasive challenge to the integrity of modern governance, justice, and societal cohesion. These singularities represent points where systems intended to serve the collective good become ensnared in their own limitations, self-interests, or ideological entrenchments. What should be the guiding hand of fairness, inclusion, and progress transforms instead into an isolating, often oppressive structure that perpetuates inequality, fragmentation, and stagnation.

The concept of the social agency singularity serves as a critical lens through which we can analyze how institutions, leaders, and societal frameworks deviate from their foundational purposes. It reveals how these deviations occur—not through overt collapse, but through subtler mechanisms of self-preservation, monopolization of power, and the manipulation of laws, norms, and language. Understanding this phenomenon is key to addressing the systemic failures that undermine the ideals of democracy, justice, and universal human rights.

The Central Themes Revisited

This book has explored numerous manifestations of singularities within social and institutional frameworks. Let us revisit the central themes that emerge:

1. The Fragmentation of Society:

Singularities thrive on isolation. Whether it is a school board operating in "embassy mode," a law enforcement body co-opting justice for its own agenda, or governance structures allowing localized groups to dictate national policy, the fragmentation of institutions erodes trust and coordination. Fragmentation prevents societies from addressing collective needs, leaving vulnerable populations even more exposed to neglect and exploitation.

2. The Subversion of Justice:

Justice is the foundation of a fair and functional society. Yet, singularities hijack the executive function of law, twisting it to serve specific ideologies or agendas. The result is selective justice, where the protections of the rule of law are unevenly distributed, and the rights of some are prioritized over others. This violates not only legal principles but also the moral underpinnings of human dignity.

3. The Role of Leadership in Singularities:

Leadership is a critical determinant in either perpetuating or breaking free from singularities. As explored in the chapter on authority figures, leaders who lack charisma, competence, or vision often rely on monopolization, oppression, and control to mask their deficiencies. Such leadership accelerates the entrenchment of singularities, as these leaders prioritize their own survival over collective progress.

4. The Redefinition of Reality:

Language and meaning are powerful tools in shaping societal structures. By redefining terms such as "privilege," "equity," or "bias," singularities alter not just the interpretation of justice but the lived reality of individuals. This redefinition creates a chasm between what laws promise on paper and what people experience daily, resulting in disillusionment and alienation.

5. The Absence of Coordinated Change:

Singularities feed on inertia. They thrive in environments where systemic reform is hindered by conflicting interests, lack of accountability, or entrenched resistance to innovation. This creates a *change singularity*, where the systems in place are incapable of adapting to new challenges, leaving society locked in a cycle of dysfunction and stagnation.

The Stakes of Breaking Free from Singularities

At its heart, this book underscores the urgency of breaking free from the grip of singularities. The stakes are immense. When institutions fail to uphold justice, fairness, and accountability, the social contract between people and their systems of governance is broken. This leads to a cascade of consequences:

- **Erosion of Trust:** Citizens lose faith in institutions, which fosters disillusionment, polarization, and social unrest.

- **Perpetuation of Inequality:** Singularities reinforce structural inequities, allowing privilege to become entrenched and denying opportunities for advancement to marginalized groups.

- **Stifling of Progress:** Societies caught in the grip of singularities are unable to innovate or respond effectively to emerging challenges, leaving them vulnerable to decline.

In the international arena, the presence of singularities also tarnishes a nation's credibility and standing. A country's adherence to the rule of law, as well as its ability to deliver justice and equality, is a cornerstone of its reputation and development. Singularities undermine these principles, perpetuating cycles of underdevelopment and global disapproval.

The Way Forward

Breaking free from singularities is not a matter of incremental change; it requires systemic transformation. This transformation must address the structural, cultural, and leadership failures that allow singularities to persist. The following steps offer a pathway toward reform:

1. Reinforcing Universal Principles:

Institutions must align their practices with universal principles such as those enshrined in the Universal Declaration of Human Rights (UDHR). No institution, regardless of its autonomy or local power, should operate outside the bounds of these principles.

2. Ensuring Accountability:

Transparency and accountability are non-negotiable. Institutions and leaders must be held accountable for their decisions, with mechanisms in place to scrutinize and correct deviations from justice and fairness.

3. Promoting Collaborative Governance:

Silos must be dismantled. The interconnectedness of institutions, leaders, and communities is essential for addressing societal challenges holistically. Collaborative governance fosters shared responsibility and coordinated action.

4. Elevating Competent Leadership:

Leadership selection must prioritize competence, vision, and integrity over convenience or nepotism. Leaders who inspire trust and mobilize collective action are essential for dismantling singularities and fostering progress.

5. Resisting the Redefinition of Reality:

Societies must remain vigilant against attempts to manipulate language and redefine justice to serve narrow interests. Safeguarding the integrity of terms and principles is critical for maintaining a shared understanding of fairness and equity.

6. Fostering a Culture of Resilience and Innovation:

Singularities thrive on stagnation. Societies must cultivate a culture of adaptability, where systems are designed to evolve and innovate in response to changing needs and challenges.

A Call to Action

The phenomenon of the social agency singularity is not an inevitable outcome; it is a choice. Societies, institutions, and individuals have the power to challenge the forces that perpetuate singularities and to demand systems that serve the greater good. This book is a call to action for leaders, policymakers, educators, and citizens to confront the entrenched systems that lock society into cycles of inequality and stagnation.

Breaking free from singularities requires courage, vision, and a collective commitment to the ideals of justice, equality, and human rights. It demands that we hold ourselves and our institutions to the highest standards, refusing to accept mediocrity or oppression as the norm. Most importantly, it requires us to believe in the possibility of change and to work tirelessly to make it a reality.

In the end, the battle against singularities is a battle for the soul of society. It is a fight to ensure that systems of governance, law, and leadership serve their true purpose: to empower individuals, advance collective progress, and uphold the dignity and rights of all. By understanding and addressing the social agency singularity, we take the first step toward building a future that fulfills the promise of justice, equality, and shared humanity.

ABOUT THE AUTHOR

My name is Ghizlane Obtel and I am a teacher with over 20 years of experience teaching at the kindergarten, elementary and high school level. I am currently teaching in Toronto, Ontario, Canada. I am also a blogger since 2016. My blogs are all focused on thinking about millennial problems and how to solve them. The thinking about civilization problem and how to make the world a better place is paramount in all my writings. Imagining the Future is a passion of mine. From technological aspects to civilization restructuring to individual character to ontology and design of new life-form. I consider myself to be a Millennial Thinker and a New Era Designer. I intend to be the époque of my time and it is reflected in all my writings. Indeed, I specialize in the worse case scenario study, breakdown, dissection and solution. This prepares Life in all its formats to face such eventualities with resolve, determination and preparedness. Or at least that is what I believe I am achieving and contributing to the success of Life through all my books and their themes.

Email: ghizlaneobtel.booksauthor@gmail.com
Blog: livingcryptonnarrative.wordpress.com

OTHER BOOKS BY THE AUTHOR

LEGAL PREMISES
IN EDUCATION
Nurturing Law-Abiding Citizens
GHIZLANE OBTEL

SOCIAL AGENCY
AS PREMISE FOR RADICALIZATION
AND TERRORISM
GHIZLANE OBTEL

MANUAL OF ENGINEERING
SOCIAL AGENCY

FOR A UNIVERSAL CIVILIZATION

GHIZLANE OBTEL

SOCIAL ADAPTATION
AND AGENCY AS EXACT
SCIENCE
GHIZLANE OBTEL

SOCIAL AGENCY SCIENCE
THE NEW UNIVERSAL
PARADIGM
GHIZLANE OBTEL

SOCIAL TRUTH
TRUTH
SOCIAL
REALITY
GHIZLANE OBTEL

ESSAYS
IN
QUANTUM
THINKING
By
GHIZLANE OBTEL

A THEORY OF THE
MIND
AND OTHER ESSAYS
IN LINGUISTICS
GHIZLANE OBTEL

THE CLASSROOM
OF THE FUTURE
The Story and Storytelling
of the Future
A Science Fiction Story
By
GHIZLANE OBTEL

CRYPTONIC
New era Design Series
Poetry Book 1
Volume 1: Paragons
By
GHIZLANE OBTEL

CRYPTONIC
ONTOLOGY
New Era Design Series
Poetry Book 1, Volume 2:
The Building Blocks
By
GHIZLANE OBTEL

CRYPTONIC
CIVILIZATION
New Era Design Series
Poetry Book 2
By
GHIZLANE OBTEL

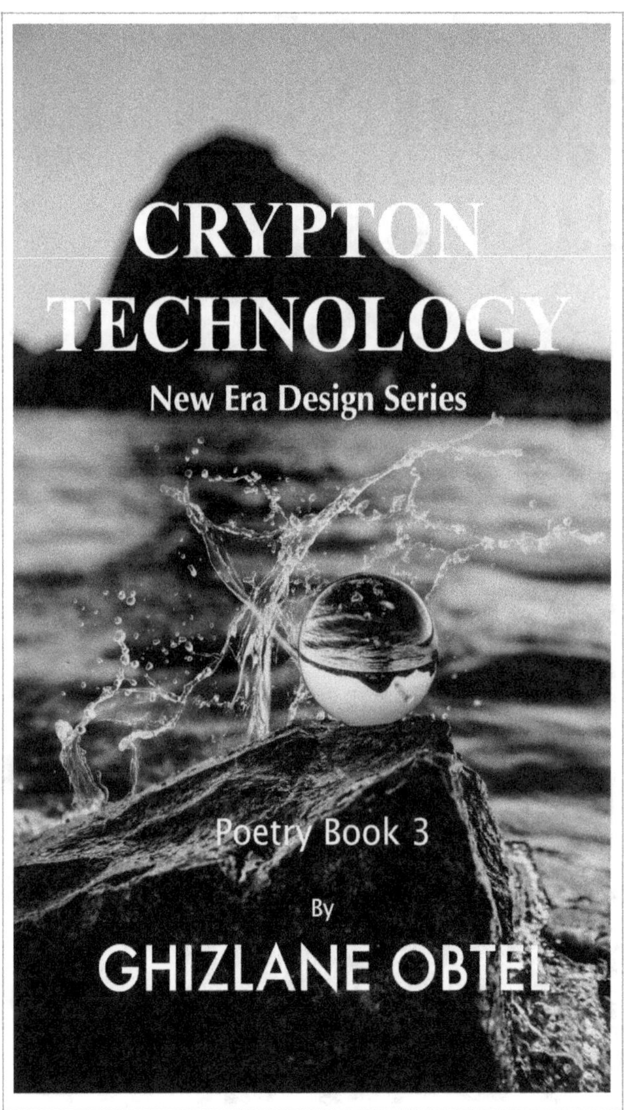

CRYPTON
TECHNOLOGY
New Era Design Series
Poetry Book 3
By
GHIZLANE OBTEL

CRYPTON
INDIVIDUAL
New Era Design Series
Poetry Book 4
By
GHIZLANE OBTEL

GHIZLANE OBTEL
Life-Drive Series
Book 1
BECOMING PHOENIX
LIFE-DRIVE ON THE RISE

DRAGON WITHIN
FIRE ESSENCE
The Story of Abstract Fire
Genesis of a New Being and Mode
GHIZLANE OBTEL
The Life-Drive Series
Book 2

GHIZLANE OBTEL
RISE
OF THE ABSTRACT PHOENIX
The Life-Drive Series
Book 3

EVER PHOENIX
EVIL DECODED
DARKNESS DECIPHERED
GHIZLANE OBTEL
The Life-Drive Series
Book 4

FATHOM
The Fathom Series
Book I
GHIZLANE OBTEL

ARCHITECT
The Fathom Series
Book 2
GHIZLANE OBTEL

ENGINEER
The Fathom Series
Book 3
GHIZLANE OBTEL

ENDLESS DAWN
OF THE EVER FREE
The Fathom Series
Book 4
GHIZLANE OBTEL

EVER FREEDOM
The Fathom Series
Book 5
GHIZLANE OBTEL

PROPOSAL
The Fathom Series
Book 6
GHIZLANE OBTEL

The Fathom Series
Book 7
STATUS
GHIZLANE OBTEL

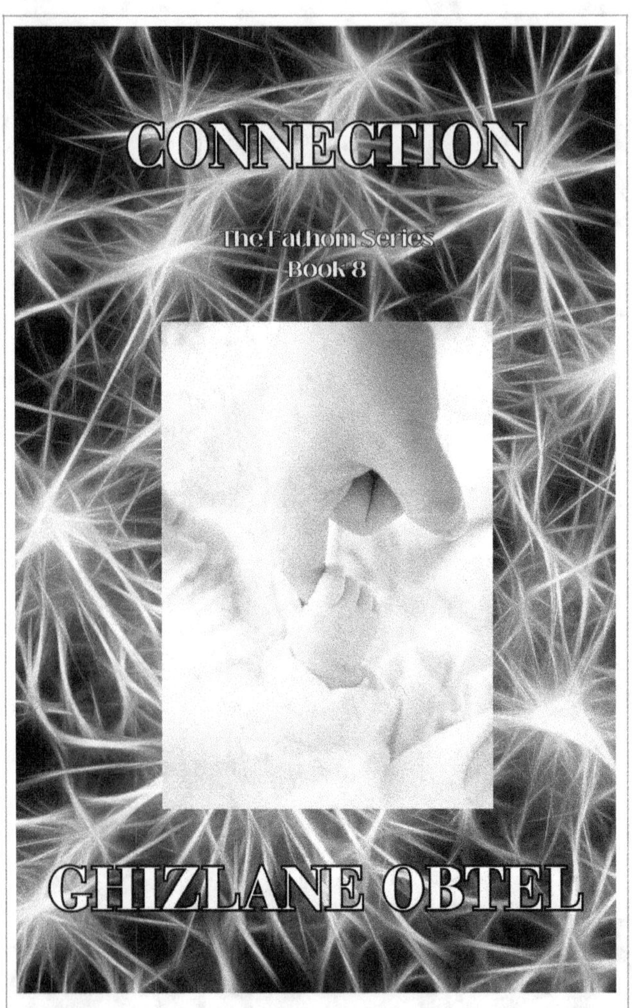

CONNECTION
The Fathom Series
Book 8
GHIZLANE OBTEL

MOTHERING
FATHOM
The Fathom Series
Book 9
GHIZLANE OBTEL